Grape Vines

By

A. Ward

British Library Cataloguing-in-Publication Data
A catalogue record for this book is available from the
British Library

Winemaking

The science of wine and winemaking is known as 'oenology', and winemaking, or 'vinification', is the production of wine, starting with selection of the grapes or other produce and ending with bottling the finished product. Although most wine is made from grapes, it may also be made from other fruits, vegetables or plants. Mead, for example, is a wine that is made with honey being the primary ingredient after water and sometimes grain mash, flavoured with spices, fruit or hops dependent on local traditions. Potato wine, rice wine and rhubarb wines are also popular varieties. However, grapes are by far the most common ingredient.

First cultivated in the Near East, the grapevine and the alcoholic beverage produced from fermenting its juice were important to Mesopotamia, Israel, and Egypt and essential aspects of Phoenician, Greek, and Roman civilization. Many of the major wine-producing regions of Western Europe and the Mediterranean were first established during antiquity as great plantations, and it was the Romans who really refined the winemaking process.

Today, wine usually goes through a double process of fermentation. After the grapes are harvested, they are prepared for primary fermentation in a winery, and it is at this stage that red wine making diverges from white wine making. Red wine is made from the must (pulp) of red or black grapes and fermentation occurs together with the grape skins, which give the wine its colour. White wine is made by fermenting juice which is made by pressing crushed grapes to extract a juice; the skins are removed and play no further role. Occasionally white wine is made from red grapes; this is done by extracting their juice with minimal contact with the grapes' skins. Rosé wines are either made from red grapes where the juice is allowed to stay in contact with the dark skins long enough to pick up a pinkish colour (blanc de noir) or by blending red wine and white wine.

In order to embark on the primary fermentation process, yeast may be added to the must for red wine or may occur naturally as ambient yeast on the grapes or in the air. During this fermentation, which often takes between one and two weeks, the yeast converts most of the sugars in the grape juice into ethanol (alcohol) and carbon dioxide. The next process in the making of red wine is secondary fermentation. This is a bacterial fermentation which converts malic acid to lactic acid, thereby decreasing the acid in the wine and softening the taste. Red (and sometimes White) wine is sometimes transferred to oak barrels to mature for a period of weeks or months; a practice which imparts oak aromas to the wine. The end product has been both revered as a highly desirous and delicious status symbol, as well as a mass-produced, cheap form of alcohol.

Interestingly, the altered consciousness produced by wine has been considered *religious* since its origin. The Greeks worshipped Dionysus, the god of winemaking (as well as ritual madness and ecstasy!) and the Romans carried on his cult under the name of Bacchus. Consumption of ritual wine has been a part of Jewish practice since Biblical times and, as part of the Eucharist commemorating Jesus' Last Supper, became even more essential to the Christian Church.

Its importance in the current day, for imbibing, cooking, social and religious purposes, continues. Winemaking itself, especially that on a smaller scale is also experiencing a renaissance, with farmers and individuals alike re-discovering its joy.

GRAPE VINES

Origin—Culture under Glass—Pot Culture—Diseases—Outdoor Culture of Vines —Propagation—Varieties—Selection of Sorts.

GRAPE VINES

ORIGIN

Vitis vinifera grows wild in the temperate regions of Western Asia, Southern Europe, Algeria, and Morocco. It is especially in the Pontus, in Armenia, to the south of the Caucasus and of the Caspian Sea, that it grows with the luxuriant wildness of a tropical creeper, clinging to tall trees, and producing abundance of fruit without pruning or cultivation. Its vigorous growth is mentioned in ancient Bactriana, Kabul, Kashmir, and even in Badak-Khan to the north of the Hindu Kush. Of course it is a question whether the plants found there, as elsewhere, are not sprung from seeds carried from vineyards by birds.

" The dissemination by birds must have begun very early, as soon as the fruit existed, before cultivation, before the migration of the most ancient Asiatic peoples, perhaps before the existence of man in Europe or even in Asia. Nevertheless, the frequency of cultivation, and the multitude of forms of the cultivated Grape may have extended naturalization and introduced among wild Vines varieties which originated in cultivation.

" The records of the cultivation of the Vine and of the making of wine in Egypt go back five or six thousand years. In the West the propagation of its culture by the Phœnicians, Greeks, and Romans is pretty well known, but to the east of Asia it took place at a late period " (*De Candolle, Origin of Cultivated Plants*).

The exceptionally wide range of temperature the Vine will not only support but actually thrive and fruit in has no parallel among domesticated races of plants. " There is a marked difference in the constitution of the several varieties, some being hardy (in England), whilst others, like the Muscat or Alexandria, require a very high temperature to come to perfection. According to Labat, Vines taken from France to the West Indies succeed with extreme difficulty, whilst those exported from Madeira or the Canary Islands thrive admirably " (*Darwin*).

The cultivation of the Vine is said to have extended from Asia to Egypt, from thence to the southern parts of Europe through Greece. From Italy it progressed northwards into France, and in all probability it had been tried in Britain by the Romans, but possibly without success; for varieties suitable for the warm climate of Italy would be likely to fail in maturing their fruit in the moist climate of our island, as indeed is stated by Tacitus to have been the case. In the year 85 Domitian prohibited by an edict the planting of new vineyards in Italy, and ordered those existing in the provinces to be destroyed. This edict was rescinded by Probus in the year 280, and Britain is particularly mentioned among the provinces which enjoyed the privilege of being allowed to cultivate the Vine. Vineyards are mentioned by Bede (before A.D. 731) as existing in several parts of Britain. In 1140 barons as well as monks possessed vineyards; by the latter, wine was made in good, and verjuice in bad seasons; and from the hardier sorts of Burgundy Grapes, planted in the most appropriate situations—and in regard to this the monks were particularly careful—a tolerably good wine may have been produced, better, no doubt, than some of the artificial champagnes of the present day.

The Vine lives to a great age under favourable circumstances. Pliny mentions one 600 years old; vines 100 years old are accounted young in the vineyards of Italy; and Bosc states there are some in Burgundy upwards of 400 years old.

The celebrated Vine at Hampton Court was planted in 1769, and despite its great age it continues to bear a large number of bunches annually. Within recent years a new border has been provided, and not only are the bunches now produced larger than formerly, but the size of the berries and finish leave nothing to be desired. There are also several other instances of Vines attaining a great age in this country, notable examples being a fine specimen of Black Hambro at

1

Cumberland Lodge, Windsor Park; one of the same variety at Eastnor Castle, Ledbury, Herefordshire; and the famous Muscat of Alexandria at Harewood House, Leeds—the latter being the largest known Vine of this variety in the kingdom. These Vines are all

alive, is said to be the parent of the Hampton Court Vine.

A Black Hambro in the garden of the Marquis of Breadalbane at Auchmore, Scotland, and known as the Kinnell Vine, occupies a house 171 feet long, and for a number of

Fig. 5.—Very old, fruitful Grape Vine at Manresa House, Roehampton

in vigorous health, and bear heavy crops of fruit annually. A Black Hambro Vine at Valentines, Ilford in Essex, which according to Gilpin was planted in 1758, and is still

years has yielded annually a crop of about 500 bunches of Grapes, ranging from 1 lb. to 3 lb. in weight. It is said to have been planted in 1832.

CULTURE UNDER GLASS

The Border.—Grapes grown on Vines in the open air generally colour well, even if they fail to ripen, and their leaves are thick and leathery. It is not always so with the foliage of Vines grown under glass, the rapidity of growth under the influence of artificial heat and moisture resulting in leaves that are generally larger, but comparatively weak and thin. Vines growing in the open air, even in this country, maintain their roots in a sound state for many years in any or-

dinary garden soil. They will do this also under glass so long as the borders are maintained in a state of efficiency.

In order that the Vines may produce regularly and support good crops of fruit for a number of years, they must be planted in properly-made borders. These should be 3 feet deep, and of the same width as the house, whether it is to be inside or outside. If partly inside and partly outside, the two portions should be of equal width (fig. 6).

In this case the front wall is built upon arches, so that the roots occupy both. The foundations for the arches should be on a level with the base of the border. Borders should be made by degrees, a portion from 3 feet to 4 feet in width each season being ample. The advantages of this plan are in its providing annually a mass of new compost for the roots to feed upon, and by the time the border is complete the whole mass of soil will be full of working roots.

A depth of 3 feet of prepared soil is not too much if on a well-drained subsoil, or a good layer of drainage not less than a foot in depth. In cold, low-lying districts the borders should be elevated above the surrounding level, and this must be taken into consideration and allowed for when constructing the houses.

Drainage.—In some situations holes may be dug to the depth of 4 feet or more without a drop of water collecting in them at any time of the year; but in others, at that depth, water will rise at almost any season, especially towards the beginning of summer, when the water-springs are at their highest. In the former case efficient drainage alone will

front, and be covered with whole turves, the grass-side downwards.

Soil.—To produce heavy crops of fruit the soil must be rich, and to prevent the roots from suffering from cold or drought it should be made up of materials not likely to become close and retentive of moisture. A rich, turfy, fibrous loam is the principal constituent, the fibre in which is of such a nature that it will not soon rot. Loams vary very much in texture, and it is not always possible to obtain that which is best suited to the growth of the Vine. A loam of poor quality may be fortified by adding burnt soil, wood ashes, road sidings, road scrapings, and ½-

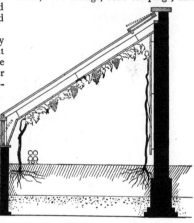

Fig. 6.—Section of Lean-to Vinery, showing Border, &c.

suffice, but in the latter it is necessary to provide a flooring of cement concrete not less than 3 inches in thickness. In both cases drains must be provided to carry off water: in the former, one laid along the front and below the bottom layer of drainage material will be sufficient, providing it has a proper fall and outlet; in the latter, the whole site of the vinery must be well drained with agricultural drain-pipes laid below the level of the concrete floor, and leading into a main drain with a good outlet.

The material for drainage should consist of three grades, the coarsest and largest to go in the bottom, the medium-sized next, and lastly the finer to finish off with. This may consist of brickbats, burrs from brick-yards, or sandstone; but whatever material is used, it must be clean and durable. The rougher portions of the drainage should be placed in position by hand, and the whole mass, when finished, should slope slightly towards the

inch bones. Heavy loams are improved by the addition of lime rubble, which ensures the requisite degree of porosity. A medium-heavy, fibrous loam should be prepared as follows: First chop the turves into rough pieces, and to every five cart-loads add one of lime rubble, one barrow-load each of charcoal, wood ashes, and fresh soot; 2 cwt. of ½-inch bones, and 2 cwt. of bone meal. For loams of a lighter nature add one cart-load of burnt soil and use less lime rubble. Farmyard manure should not be used. The whole should be thoroughly incorporated by turning it twice, leaving it in a ridge-shaped heap. Rather than allow the compost to become saturated, it is better to cover it with tarpaulins or shutters.

Planting.—This may be performed at any season, mid-winter excepted, October and February or March being the best months. Dormant canes are best for planting in an outside border. Inside, the canes may be started into growth prior to planting. Many growers plant young growing Vines, i.e. Vines raised from eyes rooted the same season. The planting must then take place later in the year, and it can only be done

Disentangle the roots after washing the soil from them in a bucket of tepid water, as shown in fig. 7; then lay them out carefully in a horizontal position, placing the topmost layer within 2 inches of the surface; cover with and shake the finest of the soil amongst them, make firm, give as much tepid water as will settle the soil closely round the roots, and finish by mulching the surface with horse droppings to a depth of 2 inches. When the border is wholly or partly inside the house, the largest proportion of the roots should be laid pointing inwards, as they have a tendency to grow towards the openings in the front wall and into the outer portion of the border. Water will not be required after planting until the Vines start into growth.

Fig. 7.—Vine prepared for planting

The distances at which to plant must be determined by the mode of training it is intended to adopt. The usual method is to confine the Vines to single stems, or rods as they are termed, and to allow a distance of 5 feet between them. If they are to be trained with two rods apiece, then 10 feet apart is not too wide. Some growers plant their permanent Vines 5 feet apart, with supernumeraries between, which, after fruiting two seasons, are cut out, as by this time the rods intended to be permanent have become established and capable of bearing good crops of fruit.

The surface of the borders requires to be frequently renewed, many growers performing this annually. This has the effect of keeping the Vines in good health by inducing the formation of fibrous feeding-roots near the surface. If this is not done, the surface soil in time becomes sour and inert from the constant application of manure and mulching, and the roots, which should be preserved and encouraged, perish. Top-dressing is therefore best done annually, and as soon as the Vines are clear of fruit.

The old soil should be carefully removed where the borders are inside. This plan has its advantages, not the least of which is that a whole season's growth is gained.

Planting should be done as follows: Open out a hole wide enough to allow of the roots being spread outwards from the stem, and so deep that when it is filled in the stem will be 1 inch deeper than it was in the pot.

with a fork, so that as few roots as possible shall be destroyed. Replace this with compost similar to that recommended for border-making, but without the bone manure, using a concentrated manure instead. Manures specially prepared for top-dressing Vine borders are to be had, and these are safe and efficacious when properly applied.

However well the borders may be constructed, in time they become exhausted. As a rule the Vines themselves indicate when this is the case by growing less vigorously, and by ceasing to produce fruit of good quality. If taken in hand as soon as the first indication is observed, matters can be rectified by a partial renewal of the border, but if left longer, the whole border must be taken out and replaced with fresh compost.

In the case of partial renewals, a strip 4 feet wide for the whole width of the border, opposite every other light, will suffice for a season or so, when the remaining portion may be dealt with. If the border is partly inside and partly outside the house, the outside portion may be renewed one season, and that inside two seasons later. In some cases entire renewal of the border is necessary. The Grapes should be ripened and used early, so that the roots can be lifted while the foliage is still green; the Vines will then make a more speedy recovery. This operation must be carried out with promptitude, so that the roots are exposed for as short a period as possible. The house should be shaded while the lifting is being performed, and the roots tied in bundles and surrounded with moss as fast as they are liberated, keeping the moss damp and syringing the Vines if the weather is sunny. Continue to shade and syringe for a few weeks after the roots have been laid out afresh, by which time new fibrils will have been formed, when shading and syringing may then be dispensed with.

Protection of Borders.—This consists of placing a layer of dry leaves about 9 inches thick on the surface of outside borders, with some litter on the top to fix them. It serves to shed off heavy rains and snow, and to prevent loss of heat. Long stable-litter also answers the same purpose. This covering should be placed on about mid-November, or, at any rate, before the borders become saturated with autumnal rains.

Forcing.—The time when a vinery should be started depends on when ripe fruit is required. For the fruit to be ripe by the beginning of May, the house should be started in the previous November, thus allowing a period of about six months. For later crops

less time is required; for instance, if a house of Black Hambro be started in February, the fruit will be ripe in from sixteen to eighteen weeks. Muscats and late-keeping kinds, such as Lady Downes, must have a longer season of growth, and be started not later than the second week in March for the crop to be finished by the end of September or early in October. Grapes thus produced can be depended on to hang well on the Vines, or to keep for a long time in the Grape-room in perfect condition.

When late-keeping Grapes are started later than the time specified, much fire-heat is necessary to ripen the fruit. This affects the flavour, which is never so rich; nor does the fruit keep so well.

Temperature.—Assuming that a vinery is to be started the first week in January, the temperature should be 45° at night and 50° in the day. When the buds have broken, increase the warmth to 50° and 55°, and as soon as the shoots are about 3 inches long further increase it to 55° and 60°. Adhere to these figures until the laterals have lengthened and the bunches begun to develop, when a further rise to 60° and 65° should take place. As soon as the Vines commence to flower, raise the temperature to 75° by day; but 65° will be ample at night.

When the fruit is set, the day and night temperatures should read 70° and 65° respectively, and continue with these figures until the fruit is properly coloured and ripe. For Muscats the temperature should be quite 5° higher than the above-named figures until the fruit is set, when a night temperature of 65° to 70° will be ample, and for the day from 75° to 80°. This treatment may be followed until the Grapes are ripe. A rise of 10° with sun-heat should in all cases be allowed for before admitting air. When the house has to be ventilated, the air should be shut off early enough to ensure the temperature rising to 85°, and even if it should exceed these figures by a few degrees no harm will be done, providing the house is damped down immediately. Avoid over-heating the hot-water pipes during cold weather; rather maintain a temperature a few degrees lower.

Ventilation.—Air should be given at all times when the state of the weather will permit, but with due caution, particularly when there is a great disparity between the internal and external temperatures. When the wind is east, especially during March and April, pieces of thin scrim or tiffany should be fastened over the ventilators to prevent rushes of cold air. If possible, avoid giving air to lower the temperature. Even if through neglect the house should be too hot, a sudden reduction of temperature by admitting cold air must not be attempted. In vineries of modern construction, where large panes of glass are used, the temperature rises quickly under the influence of the sun's rays. The attendant must therefore be on the alert, and admit a little air early in the morning, gradually increasing it as

Fig. 8.—Young Shoot of Vine, showing position of Flowers

the heat of the sun becomes more intense; there will then be no difficulty in maintaining the required temperature.

Watering and Syringing.—Heat, air, and moisture should be so regulated as to induce uniformity of growth, for on this depends not only the present but also the future crops. To obtain the requisite degree of heat and moisture in the earlier stages of growth, some growers make up a hot-bed in the body of the house. A warm, humid atmosphere, necessary to ensure an even break of the buds, is obtained by syringing the Vines several times a day, and by damping the borders, walls, and footpaths twice a day. Syringing should be discontinued after the Vines have made about 6 inches of growth. During the flowering period, damping of the floors and borders should be almost entirely sus-

pended, as a fairly dry atmosphere is essential for the free setting of the fruit. When setting is complete, the syringing and damping of all exposed surfaces in the house may be resumed at least twice a day, i.e. before admitting air in the morning and again at closing-time. On hot days the floors will need to be frequently moistened. When the fruit begins to colour, atmospheric moisture must be gradually reduced, and a dry, buoyant air maintained.

It is usual to give inside borders as much tepid water as will moisten them throughout when the house is closed for starting, unless the soil in the border is found to be sufficiently moist. Generally, however, inside borders are fairly dry when starting-time arrives. After this, watering should be done only when the roots really require it. To ascertain this, examine the soil with a subsoil-tester at different depths. Always avoid watering while the Vines are in flower.

Outside borders often do not receive the attention they should with respect to watering. It should not be performed haphazard, but only after ascertaining by means of the tester that water is actually required, and then give sufficient to moisten the border throughout and down to the drainage. A good mulch of short litter or horse droppings, spread over the surface of both inside and outside borders, obviates the necessity of frequent watering. The manure also benefits the Vines by affording food to the roots, a great help in the finishing of the crop.

Stimulants. — When Vines have become established and bear full crops of fruit, they soon exhaust the soil unless they are supplied with stimulants from time to time, either in the form of liquid manure or carefully-compounded artificial manures. The following is a powerful stimulant, of which a small quantity only is required at a time: To 1 lb. of muriate of potash add 2½ lb. of dissolved bones and 1 lb. of bone-meal. Mix all well together, and use at the rate of 2 oz. per square yard of border surface when starting the Vines, one-half of this quantity when the fruit has been thinned, and the same after the stoning period. Superphosphate of lime may be substituted for the dissolved bones, using equal quantities of the three ingredients. There are also many proprietary manures which, if used as directed, accomplish all that is claimed for them. Liquid manure may be given to old and established Vines occasionally up to the time the Grapes begin to colour.

Treatment after Planting.—Assuming that young dormant Vines are to be planted, they should be cut as low down as possible, which as a rule is level with the wall-plate. This must be done sufficiently early to prevent bleeding ensuing. Under the influence of heat and moisture the buds quickly break. When growths develop and are about half an inch long, reduce them to one on each Vine, selecting the strongest as near to the top of each cane as possible. As these lengthen, support them with sticks until they reach the trellis, afterwards keeping them regularly tied to the wires. Pinch lateral growths at the second leaf, and allow the young rods to grow unrestricted to the top of the house. If supernumeraries have been planted, stop them when they have made from 8 to 10 feet of growth, and the laterals at the first leaf.

The mode of bearing in the Vine is very different from that of many other kinds of fruit-trees. In the Peach, for example, no fruit is borne on the young shoots of the current year, but on these blossom-buds are formed for fruiting in the following season; and it can be perceived in winter where fruit will be situated in the summer, provided no accident occurs. Such is not the case with the Vine. A young rod which may grow to a length of 15 or 20 feet in a year will, when shortened to 6 or 8 feet in the autumn, develop shoots from nearly every bud when started into growth the next year. On these, as they lengthen, the rudiments of at least one bunch will be seen (fig. 8). Precisely the same thing is seen on the shoots or lateral growths on spur-pruned Vines. So whether the last year's wood is left long or pruned hard back, fruit is invariably produced. Some growers depend entirely on young rods for fruit, but generally the cutting close back of all last year's wood near to the rods, i.e. on the spurs, is the system mostly adopted.

Good crops are obtained by both methods, a proof that productiveness does not depend on any particular mode of pruning and training. For the maintenance of health and fruitfulness, that method of pruning and training should be adopted which leads to the production of the greatest amount of healthy foliage without its being crowded. The whole of the leaves should as far as possible be exposed to direct sunlight, so that the roots shall receive their due share of elaborated sap, otherwise general weakness will ensue.

Systems of Training.—Three systems of training are in use for the Vine—the long-rod, the spur, and the extension systems —which, briefly described, are as follows:—

1. The Long-rod System.—It is generally conceded that larger bunches can be obtained annually by this than by the spur system, but a greater weight of fruit results from spur-pruned Vines occupying the same extent of glass. It is seldom practised now, and only with respect to varieties which do not fruit freely on the spur system. The principle governing this method is to prune so that there shall always be a series of young rods, which, when shortened more or less according to their strength, will produce shoots and bear fruit in the current year. These rods should be cut out as soon as the Grapes have been cut. To replace them, young rods must be trained up from the base every summer, which will, in their turn, bear fruit the following season. By continuing in this way there is always a sufficiency of young fruiting rods for present needs, and at the same time all two-year-old wood is dispensed with. Long-rod training in its simplest form is accomplished as follows: Plant the Vine, train up one shoot, and when the leaves have fallen in autumn prune the young rod back to the bottom of the rafter. In the next season train up two of the strongest shoots, and when they have completed their growth, and cast their leaves, cut the weaker back to two buds. The rod left, when pruned little or much according to its strength and ripeness of wood, will furnish the crop, and should be cut out in the autumn. In the meantime, two shoots will have developed from the two buds left at the base where the other or weaker rod was shortened, which should be trained in, as the stronger will be required to replace the fruiting rod when this is dispensed with, and cut the weaker back to two buds as before.

2. The Spur System (figs. 9, 10).—This is the method most generally adopted. Assuming that a one-year-old cane has been pruned back to a length of 5 or 6 feet, and it is to be started, bend the point downwards towards the border. This is done to secure an even break of buds. When the young shoots push, tie the rod to the trellis. Then select the best-situated shoot near the tip of the rod to form a new cane, and extend the stem, pinching out the point when it has made 6 feet of growth, afterwards allowing it to grow unchecked to the top of the house.

The remainder of the shoots should be reduced, leaving the strongest and the most conveniently situated on either side of the rod about 18 inches apart. When long enough, gradually bring these side shoots, or laterals, as they are termed, to a horizontal position, and tie them to the transverse wires of the trellis. Stop them at the fifth leaf, pinch off all bunches when in the rudimentary stage, and stop sub-laterals at the first leaf. When the season's growth is completed, cut the laterals back to one bud to form the bases of spurs (see fig. 9). Then shorten the new cane to a length of 6 feet, and cut away all summer lateral growths on it. In

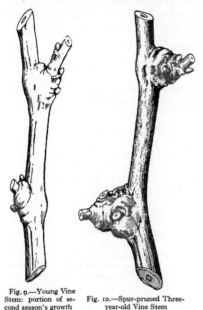

Fig. 9.—Young Vine Stem: portion of second season's growth

Fig. 10.—Spur-pruned Three-year-old Vine Stem

the season following, or second year, this cane will produce shoots which must be treated as above, leaving the best shoot to extend the rod. The lateral shoots, when pruned back to one bud in the autumn, will in turn form the bases of the spurs on that portion of the rod. The lateral growths, which at the same time push from the spurs on the lower part of the rod, should also be cut back to one bud in the autumn. If the Vines are in vigorous health, each may be allowed to bear a bunch or two on the lowermost laterals; but if supernumeraries have been planted to supply fruit in the meantime, do not allow them to bear till the next season. Pursue the same course in the next or third year, at the end of which a rod of

the required length, clothed with spurs, will have been obtained, the lower portion of which, when winter-pruned, will be similar in appearance to fig. 10.

3. The Extension System. — By this system a Vine may be trained to fill the whole of the house. Extension is really a combination of the long-rod and spur systems, as the first named has to be put into practice to lay the foundation, as it were, by filling the house with the requisite number of rods, after which the spur system is followed. While the house is being filled, temporary Vines can be made to supply fruit; these can be cut away as space is required. The usual procedure is to plant a Vine in the centre of the front of a house, if a lean-to, and at one end if span-roofed. The Vine should be cut down level with the eaves or gutter-plate, and a shoot trained out on either side parallel with it to form the base from which rods may be taken up the roof. For a span-roofed house, a single rod should be trained under the apex, and from this young rods may be trained down on either side 4 feet to 5 feet apart. Another method is to plant a Vine in each of the two extreme corners of a house, and train single rods parallel with the gutter-plate, from which rods to furnish the roof may be taken up at regular distances apart.

Disbudding.—As Vines invariably develop more growths than are required, it is necessary to reduce their number by disbudding. This is most important with young plants, as their whole future form depends on its proper performance, while established and older Vines would soon become overcrowded with growths if disbudding were not resorted to. The proper time to disbud is as soon as it can be seen how many shoots are likely to develop, and which of these it is deemed best to retain. It can be done with the finger and thumb, and without loss or check to the Vine. Many defer disbudding old Vines until they can perceive which of the laterals are carrying the best bunches, but even then the weakest and badly-placed growths should be removed as soon as they push out.

Stopping the Shoots.—As has been explained, the laterals on a two-year-old Vine and on the upper portion of a Vine in its third year should be stopped at the fifth leaf. On the lower portion of a three-year-old Vine stopping should be done at the second leaf beyond the bunch. If space is limited, it is better to do this at the first leaf than run the risk of crowding the foliage. If, on the contrary, there is ample space at command, stop them at the third leaf, for the sap, elaborated by the additional leaf, or leaves, will add vigour to the Vine. After being stopped, new growths, termed sub-laterals, will push from the axils of the leaves. Those situated between the rod and bunches are best pinched right out, but stop all others at the first leaf. Should there be room, those formed at the ends of the laterals may be left to develop two or three leaves before stopping them. Subsequent growths pushed out from these sub-laterals must be pinched at the first leaf. The leading shoots should be stopped in the manner previously mentioned, but, if there is space, stop the summer laterals at the fourth instead of the first leaf, as greater activity of the roots will, as a natural sequence, result.

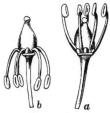

Fig. 11.—Flowers of Grape Vine (× 4)
a, Erect stamens, free setting. *b*, Deflexed stamens, shy setting.

Setting the Flowers.—Some varieties of the Vine will set well without any extraneous aid whatever, while others set badly if not assisted. Those in the first category are termed " free setters ", and in the last " bad " or " shy " setters (fig. 11). A gentle tapping or shaking of the rods suffices to cause a free dispersion of pollen in the case of free setters. In the latter instance artificial means are necessary to ensure a good set. Several expedients are adopted to accomplish this end. Some syringe the bunches when in flower, others draw their hand down them to ensure the necessary dispersion of the pollen, while others pass a pampas plume or a rabbit's tail over them. The best of artificial aids is a wide camel-hair brush. To render the operation the more successful, pollen from a free-setting sort, such as Black Hambro or Black Alicante, should be employed. Should the latter flower earlier than the varieties which have to be fertilized by hand, the pollen may be shaken or brushed into a cardboard box, and if kept dry it will retain potency for some weeks.

The adoption of these expedients is sufficient to ensure a good set of shy-setting kinds, but there are a few exceptions, which are not self-fertile, Alnwick Seedling being a notable example. Sterility arises from two causes, one of which is the deflection of the stamens from the stigma, and the other the presence of a gummy substance on the point of the stigma itself. To remove the latter, it is usual to syringe the bunches when in flower in the early morning, and when dry to fertilize the flowers at midday with pollen from another sort.

Thinning the Fruit (fig. 12).—The number of bunches left to flower and set is generally in excess of the quantity required to form the crop, so as to allow for a final selection of bunches for fruit. The number of bunches to leave depends on the health and constitution of the Vine. A safe rule is to allow 1 lb. to 1½ lb. of grapes for every foot run of rod. Thinning should take place in the case of free-setting kinds as soon as they are set, but Muscats and other sorts more difficult to set should be allowed to swell a little before they are thinned, as the more promising berries can by that time be more easily perceived.

The general form of the bunches of some sorts is that of an inverted cone, of which the stalk is the axis; in others the main stalk subdivides and forms shoulders. At the upper part of the bunch branchlets diverge from the axis, and often these again throw out stalks, bearing frequently three berries, namely, two side ones and one terminal. Towards the lower extremity of the bunch the footstalks of the individual berries proceed directly from the axis, which terminates in a single berry. In thinning, the berries which proceed directly from the axis should be first removed, then each ramification should be successively inspected, and the berries thinned out where they would otherwise be too thick, taking care to cut off those nearest the axis or central stalk. The reason of this is obvious, for if we cut off, say, two-thirds of the outer berries, those left would still be crowded; but by reversing the process the berries will then occupy a wider space, and, without unduly pressing each other, swell to their fullest extent. Therefore as many of the inner berries as can be spared should be cut out. In proceeding up the bunch, peduncles from the main axis bearing three berries, as already mentioned, will be met with; the terminal one may be left, and the two side ones removed.

The thinning of the berries should be

modified according to the varieties and the space the berries require when full-grown; and in avoiding overcrowding the bunches should not be made too thin. Moreover, the berries should not be touched either with head or hands that are perspiring. As they increase in size after the first thinning, the bunches should be looked over, and regulated by a second thinning. After the berries have

on to the nearest training-wire or lateral, so as to elevate or spread out the portion of the bunch to which it is attached. This may be done and undone much more rapidly than a tie.

Keeping the Grapes.—When the fruit becomes ripe in the early houses it can, if required, be kept in good condition for some considerable time if the following simple

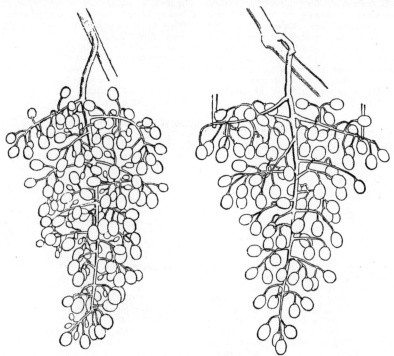

Fig. 12.—Young Bunches of Grapes
1, Before, and 2, after thinning.

stoned and taken the final swelling, they should be again examined, in case any should be in danger of wedging at the finish.

Where there are shoulders, they should be tied away from the main part of the bunch, and then thinned. A readier mode of suspending the shoulders of large bunches is by means of convenient lengths of fine wire, such as is used for mounting flowers for bouquets, bent at each end into the form of a crook, one end being hooked in near the end of the shoulder, and the other hooked

conditions are observed: The house should be kept cool, the floors damped down on hot, bright days, and the borders kept in an equable state of moisture—the reverse conditions cause shrivelling. Unless the Vines are well furnished with foliage, a slight shading of the roof will be beneficial, as black Grapes when fully ripe soon lose colour if exposed to direct sunshine.

More care is needed with regard to the keeping of late Grapes. These should be ripe about the end of September.

POT CULTURE

Vines for fruiting in pots should be raised from eyes, and be grown on as strongly as possible. When the young plants have filled the pots with roots, give them a shift into 6-inch or 8-inch pots, and from these into the fruiting-pots, which should be 12 inches or 14 inches in diameter. For compost use the best fibrous loam obtainable, chopped moderately fine. With each barrow-load mix a 10-inch potful of bone-meal, a little

growth they require a brisk temperature and an abundance of atmospheric moisture. Some apply a brisk bottom-heat to the pots after the first shift, but we think they are best grown without its aid once they are shifted into fruiting-sized pots. While in full growth the night temperature may range from 65° to 70°, and from 75° to 80° by day, allowing a further rise of 10° with sun-heat. Close the house as early as is consistent with

Fig. 13.—Pot-grown Vines

charcoal broken to the size of cob-nuts, or wood ashes, and a little well-rotted manure quite free from worms. Wash the pots, and place 2 inches of crocks in the bottom, sprinkling a little fine soot among them before covering them with pieces of rough turf. The potting is best done in the house in which the Vines are growing, to avoid risk of chill, and if the compost is taken in a few days before the potting takes place, it will get warm by the time it is wanted. These precautions should always be taken with young Vines.

When the Vines commence to make new

safety; ply the syringe vigorously on plants, walls, paths, &c. As growth proceeds, train the plants as single canes tied to the wire trellis under the roof. Until the shoots reach the trellis, stake them and attend to the tying. When the canes are from 6 to 8 feet long, pinch out the ends. Lateral shoots will then push, and these must in turn be stopped at the first leaf as fast as they appear. From the time they begin to make new roots, they must be watered freely; they should also have liquid manure when the pots have become filled with roots. Mulchings of short manure or horse droppings will also

11

be beneficial, as they serve both to feed the roots and to a great extent check too rapid evaporation from the soil.

When the canes show signs of becoming ripened, i.e. when the bark turns brown, less atmospheric moisture and more air will be required, reducing it by degrees, so that the house can eventually be freely ventilated both by day and by night. Continue to give the

fruiting size in the first season, to rear them with less heat, and to fruit them after they have made the second year's growth. In this case it is unnecessary to shift them the first year after they have been put into 6-inch or 8-inch pots. In the winter following propagation, cut back the young canes to within three eyes of the soil. When the canes are started into growth (which should take place

Fig. 14.—A well-fruited Pot-grown Vine

same amount of attention to root waterings, and as soon as the ripening of the canes is complete, cut away all lateral growths, and prune back each cane to the desired length. Then place them in the open air against a south wall, or hedge, to get thoroughly ripened. Protect the roots in the pots by standing boards in front of the latter, or otherwise placing some long litter round and about them, and always give them all the water they require.

Another method of growing pot Vines is, instead of raising and growing them on to a

early in February), shake them out, and re-pot in as small pots as the roots can conveniently be got into, and grow them on as already advised; select the strongest of the three breaks to form the future cane, rubbing off the other two. When well grown, such plants are much stronger and more robust than those grown in one year.

Fruiting Vines in Pots.—About the middle of November, earlier or later according to the urgency of the demand for early Grapes, the Vines should be placed in the house or pit in which they are to be forced. The pots may be plunged in manure or tan having a temperature of 70° to 75°, or they may be fruited quite as satisfactorily if the pots are merely stood on boards, or a stage placed over the hot-water pipes near the front of the house. The temperatures already given with regard to forcing the Vine will apply here, as will also other directions for general management.

To ensure an even break of buds, pot Vines should always have the apex of the canes bent round to a point below the rims of the pots, and be well syringed three or four times a day. When well started, the canes may be re-tied to the trellis and disbudded as soon as it can be seen which of the shoots are showing the best bunches, stopping those retained at the second leaf beyond the bunch. Keep the air rather dry when the Vines are in flower, and fertilize with a camel-hair brush. Reduce the number of bunches as soon as the fruit is set and swelling, and then start thinning.

The number of bunches to leave on each Vine must be governed by its strength. As a rule six bunches are sufficient, and on the strongest canes the number should never exceed eight. By this time the roots will require plenty of moisture and rich food, both liquid and solid, applying the latter in the form of top-dressings. In all other respects the cultural treatment is the same as that recommended for Vines in borders. A good example of a Vine fruited in a pot is shown at fig. 14.

For the preparation of Grapes for exhibiting, &c., see p. 88.

DISEASES

The Vine is peculiarly susceptible to diseases of various descriptions, the chief of

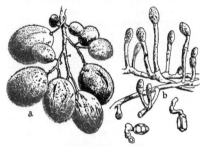

Fig. 15.—*a*, Mildew of Grapes (*Oidium Tuckeri*); *b*, conidia; *c*, conidia germinating (× 160).

which are as follows: Mildew (*Oidium Tuckeri*). This is often very destructive, both in vineries and in the open air, not only in this country but in France, Germany, Italy, and the Greek Archipelago. It appears to the naked eye like a white powder, but seen under the microscope it consists of a network of white branching filaments, from which others, either resembling a club or necklace in shape, arise almost in a perpendicular direction; and by the spores and utricles of these the fungus is rapidly propagated. The principal causes of mildew in Vineries is a too low temperature, accompanied by a very damp atmosphere; a less frequent cause being the admitting of air during the prevalence of cold, easterly winds. Therefore, in Vineries liable to attack, a warm, buoyant atmosphere should be maintained by keeping the hot-water pipes constantly heated, admitting air with caution, not opening the front lights until the stoning period is past, and syringing and damping down only when necessary. Should these measures fail, the most effectual agent for the destruction of mildew is sulphur, applied by some means in the form of a vapour. To a certain extent this can be done if, after heating the hot-water pipes to such a degree that the hand can barely be held on them, they are painted with sulphur previously made into a paste. The heat should continue for an hour, and then be shut off. This should be done three evenings in succession. A more effectual way is to employ a sulphur vaporizer (fig. 135). The vapour given off by this apparatus is most destructive to mildew, but does no harm either to fruit or foliage. When vaporizing is necessary, abstain from syringing and damping both in the morning and afternoon on every occasion.

By the liberal use of sulphur in one year there is little danger of an attack in the following season, but it is always best to adopt preventive measures early in the season. After being pruned, the Vines should be washed with water in which some soft soap has been dissolved, and afterwards dressed with a mixture of soft soap and sulphur, made by first dissolving ½ lb. soft soap in 4 gallons of hot water, and afterwards adding 3 lb. flowers of sulphur. Every portion of the wood should be painted with this mixture.

Shanking.—This term is applied to a

physiological defect, in consequence of which the stalks of the immature fruit lose their green colour, and shrivel before the berries are ripe. It has been assigned to various causes, such as cold borders, over-cropping, injudicious denudation of foliage; but the most frequent cause of all is the roots getting down into the cold subsoil. The only remedy in that case is to lift the Vines, and, to avoid future trouble, concrete the base before putting in a new border.

Rust.—This is the result of injury to the skin of the berries while they are young and

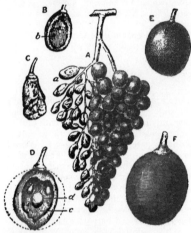

Fig. 16.—Scalded Grapes

A, Bunch of Lady Downes (reduced); *a*, scalded size.
B, Partly scalded berry; *b*, scalded portion.
C, Shrivelled berry, after scalding.
D, Partly scalded berry; *c*, shrunken patch; } All nat. size.
  d, seeds.
E, Sound berry at time of scalding.
F, Perfectly finished berry.

tender. It is often caused by cold, cutting draughts, the result of admitting air on bright mornings early in the season when the wind is blowing from the east; and less frequently by overheating the hot-water pipes, especially if there should be any sulphur left on the latter from the previous season; and by the hands, arms, or hair coming in contact with the berries while the thinning is being done. The ventilators of a span-roofed house should be opened on the opposite side to that from which the wind is blowing, or, if a lean-to, fasten something over the openings to temper the inrush of the cold outer air.

Scalding (fig. 16).— This is oft-times caused through vineries being allowed to become too hot on bright mornings before

admitting air, but generally while the Grapes are stoning, more particularly when little or no fire-heat is made use of during the night. The berries then become cold, and when the sun raises the temperature in the early morning, moisture condenses on them, with the result that, unless the ventilators are carefully manipulated, scalding takes place. The best means to adopt for its prevention is to keep a little heat in the hot-water pipes and a chink of air on the top ventilators throughout the night, also by damping down somewhat less than usual at closing-time. Lady Downes's Seedling is very liable to scalding whilst stoning.

Diptheritis.—This disease is not of frequent occurrence, but when an attack is set up a considerable loss of young growths and leaves ensues, both on old and young Vines. Its presence is denoted by the partly developed leaves on the affected shoots turning brown at their margins, and as the disease progresses they become contracted and finally die. The tips of the shoots then die off, and the lower portion afterwards becomes more or less affected with the malady. There is no known remedy. The only thing that can be done is to promptly cut off and burn the infected shoots.

Black Rot, although a destructive disease, is seldom troublesome in this country. The leaves are first attacked, reddish-brown spots appearing, which ultimately run together and form large blotches on their surfaces. On these, small black spots appear, which contain the spores of *Phoma*. These when mature disperse, and infection of the berries follows. Small discolorations of the skin are then seen, these being of a reddish-brown colour, which quickly spread. Then minute black specks appear, and finally the affected berries turn black and shrivel up. The remedy for this disease is to spray the Vines, before and after they have flowered and set their fruit, with Bordeaux Mixture. It is also wise to spray again after the Grapes are cut.

Rot.—A disease caused by *Rosellinia necatrix*, a destructive fungus found on the roots of the Vine and of numerous other plants. It works entirely in the soil, attacking and killing rootlets and roots. There is no known cure for it, but as it thrives best in wet, badly-drained soils, the preventive measures to be adopted with respect to the Vine will be those of good drainage, and care in the preparation of the border, seeing that everything likely to breed fungus is excluded from the compost. As a rule the foliage gives indication by flagging that something is amiss. Infected roots are more or less damaged by the mycelium of the fungus. As the mischief is generally done before the cause is discovered, there is no remedy other than the renewal of both Vines and border.

Spot.—Some varieties of Grapes, Muscats especially, are subject to a peculiar disorder, known as " Spot ", which affects the berries prior to the stoning stage being reached. The berries will on one side, to all appearances, seem as if they had sustained a slight bruise, and as they grow larger this portion ceases to swell, with the result that when fully grown they look to be lop-sided. It is generally considered that " Spot " is caused by chills, such as may follow a sudden inrush of cold air where the opening of the ventilators is neglected until the temperature has become abnormally high. Those disfigured berries are, when possible, best cut out.

Warts on the Leaves.—The wart-like growths found on the backs of Vine leaves are caused through a rupture of the epidermis. This is invariably due to the maintenance of high temperatures, accompanied

with a saturated atmosphere. They are undoubtedly injurious, as respiration, as a result, is impeded. Preventives are to ventilate more freely, and to perform less damping, especially in the front part of the house in the early morning.

Bleeding.—This generally results from not pruning until late in the season. The sap exudes from the wounds caused by the pruning. The wounds should be dressed with a styptic as soon as pruning is completed. Repeated applications of " painter's knotting " will generally arrest bleeding.

Adventitious Roots.—These are usually taken to be an indication either that the roots are inactive or that a too moist atmosphere is maintained. In the latter case the remedy is obvious. In the former, lifting the Vines and a partial renewal of the border is a sure remedy.

Insects, &c.—See article on INSECT AND OTHER PLANT ENEMIES. *Bark Enemies*— Mealy Bug, Vine Scale. *Fruit and Seed Enemies*—Grape Moth, Mice, Rats, Wasps. *Leaf Enemies*—Black Vine Weevil, Clay-coloured Vine Weevil, Red Spider, Thrips. *Root Enemies*—Vine Louse (*Phylloxera*).

OUTDOOR CULTURE OF VINES

The cultivation of Grape Vines in the open in the British Isles has been almost entirely superseded by that of glass-house treatment. We still see a few cottages and farmsteads with their front walls and gables covered with Vines, but it is only under good management and in warm situations that they produce fruit worth eating, even when the weather conditions are favourable.

Soil.—Provided the situation is warm and sunny, and the roots are supplied with a moderate amount of moisture, the Vine will grow in almost any soil. It succeeds both in strong, deep loam and in rocky ground thinly covered with poor sandy soil. The best soil, perhaps, is a rich, mellow loam, and it should be renewed occasionally with a top-dressing of maiden loam and manure.

Planting.—The best time to plant Vines against walls or elsewhere in the open air is in October or November, or in spring just before growth commences. The roots should be carefully spread out and covered with turfy loam in a fine condition, then well watered, and afterwards mulched.

Pruning and Training.—This is carried out much on the same principle as that which

obtains under glass. For walls of good height the Vines should be trained on the extension system, cutting a young cane back to within 18 inches of the ground, and

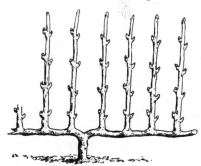

Fig. 17.—Method of Training Vine against Wall in the Open Air (Winter)

in the following season training two shoots horizontally, one to the right and one to the left. In the autumn shorten them to 5 or 6 feet, according to strength. When the buds break in the next year, retain young

Fig. 18—Vineyard on the Marquis of Bute's Estate, Castell Coch, South Wales

shoots at a distance of 18 inches apart, and pull off the surplus. Train these young shoots vertically, as shown in the figure, and in the autumn cut all back to a length of 5 or 6 feet. When the buds develop, leave one shoot on either side of each at a distance of 18 inches apart, and one at the tips with which to extend the rods. The side shoots, when pruned back to one bud, will form the bases of the future spurs, and from these shoots will push in the year following which will bear fruit. These should be stopped at the second leaf beyond the bunch.

When the wall on which the Vine is to be trained does not exceed 8 or 10 feet in height, the main rods or stems should be trained horizontally instead of in a vertical direction. This is effected by the adoption of the same principle of pruning and training as is practised with regard to fruit trees when grown as espaliers.

The cultivation of the Vine is perhaps nowhere so carefully practised as at the village of Thomery, on the banks of the Seine, about 5 miles from Fontainebleau, and from this neighbourhood Paris is supplied with 30,000 lb. of Grapes daily during the Grape season.

A vineyard of the French pattern for the open-air cultivation of Grapes for wine-making was formed by Lord Bute at Castell Coch, near Cardiff, in 1875. The Vines were planted in rows a yard apart each way, and trained to stakes 4 feet high. In favourable seasons they yield good crops of fruit, from which excellent wine was made. The variety grown was Gamay Noir.

PROPAGATION

The vine is propagated either by seeds, cuttings, eyes, layers, or grafts.

Seeds.—This method is resorted to only with the view of obtaining new varieties. If the petals of the flowers of the Vine are ex-amined, it will be observed that they are inflected at the top, and form a kind of case enclosing the stamens and pistil. When the Vine is in good health, and growing in a suitable temperature, this cap is thrown off, and the anthers exposed to the influence of light and air; they then soon burst, and the pollen escapes, some of which falls upon the stigma, and fertilization is effected. When crossing is to be performed, the stamens before they burst should be cut away with a pair of fine-pointed scissors; and afterwards, when the stigma is sufficiently developed, indicated by the stickiness of the surface, it should be covered by means of a camel-hair pencil with the pollen from a flower of the variety intended to be the male parent. The seeds that result should be saved and sown early in February, in pots or pans filled with light, rich loam, mixed with a little leaf-mould, in bottom-heat. Pot the seedlings as soon as they are in fit condition, and grow them on in heat. They may, if thought desirable, be inarched on Vines already established, with the view of proving their merits the more quickly. If means are not at command for doing this, grow them on in pots, when they will fruit either the second or third year.

Cuttings.—Where the soil is warm, well-ripened Vine shoots inserted in the open ground will strike root; but in this climate the progress is too slow for a good shoot to be formed before cold weather sets in. With bottom-heat the rooting process is accelerated, but it is found, notwithstanding, that when a young shoot is produced with plenty of air and sufficient moisture, the returning sap is checked considerably when it comes to the old wood, and we frequently see that the young shoot becomes in consequence thicker than the old wood intervening between it and the roots. Such being the case, it is found best in propagating the Vine to dispense as much as possible with the old wood.

Eyes.—Plants raised from cuttings formed of single eyes or buds are generally preferred. A node cut from a thoroughly ripened cane, with a plump bud and half an inch of wood on either side, is all that is necessary; but many go farther, and slice off half the wood opposite the bud, as a further inducement to the more rapid formation of roots. The eyes should be planted early in January, and singly in small pots, filled with a compost consisting of good friable loam, leaf-mould, and sand. They ought then to be kept in moderate heat for a week, and afterwards plunged in a propagating-case, or hot-bed, having a bottom-heat of 75°. When the cuttings have made roots and growth, as shown in fig. 19, bottom-heat may be increased to 85°, the top-heat averaging about the same by day and 75° by night. As soon

as the roots have reached the sides of the pots, give the plants a shift into larger-sized pots, which, unless the Vines are intended for forcing the next season, need not exceed 7 inches in diameter. By the time the plants are ready for shifting they will be growing freely, and by affording them the right degree of top- and bottom-heat, with plenty of light, air, and moisture, as well as occasional waterings with clear liquid manure, or weak guano-water, strong, well-rooted plants, with firm wood, superior to those raised from cuttings and other means, will be ensured by the end of the season.

Another method of raising Vines from eyes is by inserting each eye singly in pieces

Fig. 19.—Eye-cutting when rooted

of turf a few inches square, placed closely together in a propagating-case, or on a hot-bed. As soon as plenty of roots have been formed, each plant should be potted off and grown on in precisely the same manner afterwards as advised above.

Layering.—By this mode it was formerly usual to propagate the Vine in the open ground, and strong plants were produced by the end of the first season. Layering is but little practised now, and then only when it is desirable to fill part or the whole of a house with rods of the same variety. To accomplish this, take an established Vine possessing sufficient flexibility to be bent round and brought down to the surface of the border without sustaining damage. Then open out a narrow trench in the border, and of sufficient depth that the rod may be buried just below the surface. A few strong pegs will be necessary to hold the rod in position, and when this has been done, cover with soil. When the buds break, all that is necessary is to select the required number of rods from among the strongest and most conveniently placed of the young shoots issuing from the spurs, and rub all others off. In a short space of time an abundance of roots will be emitted from each spur, and by the end of

Fig. 20.—Grafting the Vine

the season the entire length of the old rod will have become firmly rooted, and the roof furnished with strong healthy rods. This method of layering is practicable only when the borders are situated inside the vinery.

Grafting.—The grafting of Vines is easily and successfully accomplished, provided the operation is performed when both stock and scion are in a fit state. When vegetation is inactive, no vital union can take place; and, on the other hand, if the Vine is wounded when the sap is rising, and before the leaves expand, bleeding ensues. Having at the time of pruning selected scions from the best-matured shoots of the kind it is intended to propagate, let their ends be inserted in pots filled with moist earth and stand outdoors until required. In the meantime the stock or branch intended to be worked should be cut back to where the graft is to be put on, doing this before there is any danger of bleeding likely to occur. The grafting may be done either on last year's wood or that which is older, taking care, however, to see that a bud is situated just below where the cut is made. Cut back the stock to where the scion can be conveniently put on; the best method is that termed " whip " grafting.

When the buds begin to grow on the Vines to be grafted, introduce the scion into a similar temperature to that in which the stock is growing, so that they may start the quicker after grafting. When the terminal bud on the stock has pushed and made four or five leaves, pinch it back to two leaves, and then insert the scion on the opposite side of the stock (fig. 20), taking care not to injure the pinched-back shoot, as the loss of this will result in the scion failing to grow. Bind the scion on tightly with raffia, leaving the bud free to push, and when completed smear with grafting-wax to exclude air. As soon as the buds of the scion have fairly expanded into leaf, and growth becomes vigorous, the shoot on the stock may be gradually removed. If the grafting has been properly performed, the union will be complete in from four to six weeks, when the ties may be cut. The shoot from the graft, if allowed full freedom, will make rods from 15 to 20 feet long the first year.

Fig. 21.—Bottle-grafting

Another method is that known as bottle-grafting (fig. 21). This should be performed soon after the stock has started into growth. The scion should be from 9 to 12 inches in length, and at about the middle of it a slice cut out about 5 inches long, taking care that there is a good bud at or near the top of it. Then cut a corresponding piece out of the stock, fit the two carefully, and bind them tightly together in the usual way, covering with grafting-wax. From 2 to 3 inches of the scion should project above, and from 4 to 5 inches below the binding. The piece below must be placed in a bottle filled with water, and suspended from the trellis or fixed in any convenient position, and be filled up as often as required. The scions usually root freely in the water in the bottles, but the roots generally die when the bottle is removed, which may be any time after the young rods have made from 10 to 12 feet of growth. The portion of the scion which was in the bottle may be pruned away either soon after there is no further need for the latter, or in the winter months, it being immaterial which.

Inarching, or grafting by approach, is another method of propagation frequently adopted to test the merits of a new variety, or to change the variety without removing the old plants. The scion is usually a young Vine in a pot, which is started into growth along with the stock, so that growth on both shall be of about equal strength. When the shoots have developed from four to five leaves, the inarching is done by cutting a slice of the green wood off the scion, and a corresponding piece off the shoot on the stock, fitting them together, and binding with raffia (fig. 22). In the course of ten days or a fortnight the union will be complete, when the ties should be removed and replaced again rather loosely,

as a protective measure in case of accident. When growth becomes vigorous, the scion below the point of union may be gradually cut away, as the stock will supply all the

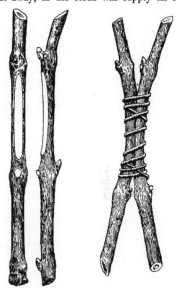

Fig. 22.—Grafting by Approach

nourishment required to enable the young shoot to develop. All growth on the stock should be persistently pinched back, so that its energies may be concentrated on the production of what will ultimately become the future Vine.

VARIETIES

The varieties of Grapes are exceedingly numerous; the following are some of the best for cultivation in this country, either on the open wall or under glass:—

ALICANTE (fig. 23).—Leaves large, leathery, downy beneath. Growth vigorous, moderately fruitful. Bunches very large, broadly shouldered; stalk short and stout; very free setting. Berries large oval, jet black, and densely covered with a bluish bloom; skin tough. Flesh tender, juicy, slightly red, of indifferent flavour unless well-ripened. It is a decidedly late Grape, second to Lady Downes in keeping qualities, and succeeds best when grown with it. It is easily cultivated, and may be grown in a cool house most successfully, where it colours to perfection, but the flavour is then only third rate.

ALNWICK SEEDLING (Clive House Seedling) (fig. 24).—Leaves large, green, much serrated,

and handsomely coloured in the autumn immediately before falling. Habit vigorous, growth strong, and extremely fruitful. Supposed to be a seedling from a cross between Black Morocco and Syrian. A very fine Grape of easy cultivation that will keep in fine conditon for a long time after it is ripe. Should be grown in the coolest end of the latest vinery if required for winter use. The only drawback to this otherwise fine variety is that it is a bad setter, and great care is needed in the setting, otherwise a crop of nothing but small and seedless berries will result. If the flowers are syringed in the early morning, the gummy exudation at the points of the stigmas, which is the cause of sterility incidental to this variety, is washed off. At midday fertilize the bunches with pollen collected on a camel-hair brush from a free-setting kind. By adopting these means a very heavy set may be ensured. Bunches large, often irregularly formed, heavily shouldered, some-

Fig. 23.—Grape—Alicante

Fig. 24.—Grape—Alnwick Seedling

Fig. 25.—Grape—Black Hambro

times long, often short and conical; berries large, roundish, sutured down one side; skin thick, tough, deep-black, covered with a copious blue bloom; flesh firm, purplish; flavour rich, and much resembling that of Black Hambro. The flavour is much enhanced by working it on the Muscat; the bunches then come longer and more tapering.

APPLEY TOWERS.—A fine black Grape of recent introduction; highly esteemed by many growers for its late-keeping qualities. Bunch large-shouldered, symmetrically formed; berries medium to large, roundish-oval; skin thick, black, covered with a blue bloom; flesh tender, juicy, and richly flavoured when well ripened. Should be grown to succeed Black Hambro; also in the late house for mid-winter supply. Was raised at Appley Towers, Isle of Wight.

BLACK CLUSTER (Black Burgundy, Early Black, Small Black Cluster).—Leaves nearly smooth, rather deeply lobed, but having shallow serratures. Bunch small and compact; berries rather small, roundish-oval; skin deep-black, thick; flesh sweet, juicy, and rich. This is a very old variety, and one of the hardiest known. In this country its wood becomes firmer and better matured in the open air than that of any other kind.

BLACK FRONTIGNAN.—Leaves roundish, sharply serrated, but not deeply lobed; midribs smooth. Bunch medium to large, tapering, frequently shouldered; berries small, round; skin blue-black, covered with an abundant bloom, thin in texture; flesh firm, juicy, with a rich Muscat flavour, on which account this Grape should be included in every collection.

BLACK HAMBRO (fig. 25).—Leaves large, with three principal lobes, the middle one tapering and elongated, smooth above, slightly pubescent beneath; footstalks long. Bunches medium to large, broadly shouldered; berries large, round and occasionally oval, when highly fed oblate, measuring less from the stalk to the opposite end than transversely; skin black, covered with a copious bloom, rather thick, unless allowed to hang till at the point of commencing to shrivel. It is only then that the fruit is perfectly ripe and the flesh acquires to its fullest extent its rich and delicious flavour; indeed it may be affirmed that nine-tenths of the produce of this excellent variety is consumed when only well coloured, and even in that state is considered good. A bunch of Black Hambro has been grown by Mr. Hunter, of Lambton Castle, which weighed 21 lb. 12 oz.

BLACK MOROCCO (Black Muscadel).—Leaves very deeply lobed, the lobes overlapping the broad open sinuses; very beautiful when dying off in autumn. Bunch very large, long and regularly shaped, and shouldered; berries large, oval, black; pulp firm and sweet. A noble-looking Grape, but a shy setter. It should be fertilized with the pollen of Hambro or Alicante, and grown in a Muscat house. A robust grower, but somewhat shy of producing bunches if too closely pruned.

BLACK MUSCAT OF ALEXANDRIA (Muscat Hambro) (fig. 26).—Leaves large, three-lobed, nearly smooth above, pubescent beneath, the ribs set with short bristly hairs. Bunch very long, tapering, and shouldered, oft-times setting badly, and much given to shanking; berries large, oval or roundish-oval, black; skin thin; flesh of the consistence of Black Hambro, very rich, and when fully ripened of true Muscat flavour. This fine Grape appears to have almost gone out of cultivation until about 1848, when, with the increased skill of modern

practice, examples of it produced as a supposed new Grape by Mr. Snow of Wrest Park again brought it into notice, since which time it has been highly esteemed by many cultivators. It is both free-growing and fruitful, especially when grafted either on Black Hambro or Muscat of Alexandria, and fertilized with the pollen of a free-setting variety when in flower. Will succeed either in a Muscat house or with Black Hambro.

BLACK PRINCE.—Leaves lobed, generally overlapping, pubescent, the ribs slightly bristled, dying off purple in the open. Bunches very long and tapering, occasionally shouldered; stalk long; berries medium, oval, bluish-black, covered with a copious bloom; flesh white, purplish under the skin, juicy, and rich in flavour, but not equal to

Fig. 26.—Grape—Black Muscat of Alexandria

Black Hambro. It is a free-bearing, vigorous-growing variety; valuable for early forcing, as the berries always colour well. Will succeed in the open air in warm situations.

BOWOOD MUSCAT. — Bunch large-shouldered; stalks green, differing in this respect from those of Muscat of Alexandria, which are tinged with red; berries very large, oval or obovate, deep-amber when fully ripe; flesh firm, juicy, with a rich, sugary, Muscat flavour. It requires the same cultural treatment as Muscat of Alexandria, is a more free setter than it, while it has the merit of keeping equally long and well. Raised at Bowood, from Canon Hall and Muscat of Alexandria.

BUCKLAND SWEETWATER.—Bunches very large-shouldered, sometimes unsymmetrical in appearance; berries large, round, and occasionally hammered; skin thin, golden or amber when ripe, otherwise pale-green; flesh melting, juicy, and richly flavoured. This is one of the best white Grapes other than Muscat. It is rather later in starting than Black Hambro, and should be grafted on that variety. It ripens with Hambro, and requires precisely similar treatment; does not set its berries quite so freely, and when forced early should be fertilized by hand when in flower. It is not adapted for late work.

CALABRIAN RAISIN.—Leaves not deeply lobed, smooth above and below, even the ribs being glabrous, instead of being furnished with short bristly hairs, as are those of most other varieties. Bunch large, very long and shouldered; berries round, white, thinly covered with a delicate bloom, transparent, so that the seeds can be seen; flesh firm, sweet and pleasant, though not rich. The bunch is of handsome proportions when highly cultivated, and although a Grape of third-rate quality, is deserving of being included in the late vinery, as the fruit hangs in excellent condition to a late period.

CANON HALL MUSCAT. — This variety has thicker shoots, larger and more tapering bunches,

Fig. 27.—Grape—Diamond Jubilee

and larger berries than Muscat of Alexandria. In point of flavour Canon Hall is rather the inferior of the two. Is a bad setter, and must be fertilized by hand with foreign pollen. When well set the bunches are remarkably handsome in appearance, and the berries attain an enormous size. As it is so capricious, the variety is not extensively cultivated in private gardens. Is much grown in the Channel Islands for market. Was raised at Canon Hall in Yorkshire.

CHASSELAS NAPOLEON. — A very handsome Grape deserving extended cultivation. Is of a robust constitution, having leaves of a pale-green colour. Bunches large, broad-shouldered, and well formed. Berries large, oval; skin tough, white, or with high cultivation, golden; flesh firm, juicy, of sweet flavour. The fruits should be freely exposed to the light. Heat is required to bring out its good qualities.

DIAMOND JUBILEE (fig. 27).—A cross between Gros Colmar and Gros Maroc. Bunches long,

well-formed, conical, averaging from 2 lb. to 3 lb. in weight. Berries oval, very large, black, coated with blue-black bloom; skin thick; flesh firm, juicy, flavour first-rate when well ripened. Is of easy cultivation, very free-setting and fruitful. It is more suited for mid-season and late rather than for early supply, and is a first-rate market Grape. For exhibition purposes it holds a high position. It is quite distinct from Black Morocco.

DIRECTEUR TISSERAND.—Of recent introduction, and when better known will be greatly esteemed. The berries resemble those of Alnwick Seedling, but it sets more freely than that variety. The bunches are medium-sized, conical in form, and handsome. Berries medium to large, roundish-oval; skin dense black, covered with a heavy bloom; flavour sweet and refreshing. Is a fine late-keeping Grape and a good exhibition variety.

DUKE OF BUCCLEUCH.—Bunches large, ovate, broadly shouldered; berries very large, round, inclining to oblate; skin thin, of a fine golden colour when well finished and ripe; flesh melting, with a very abundant juice; flavour quite distinct, and extremely rich and pleasant. This noble-looking Grape was raised by the late Mr. W. Thomson, of Clovenfords, Galashiels, who not only grew it extensively for market, but succeeded in bringing out all its good qualities better than any other grower. It is an early Grape, and will not hang long after ripening. Succeeds best grown on the long-rod system, and requires to be fertilized by hand to ensure perfect fructification.

FOSTER'S SEEDLING (fig. 28). — This is an excellent white Grape, much superior to Royal Muscadine, and, being equal to it in flavour, has superseded that good old sort for culture under glass. It is also one of the best Grapes for pot culture. Sets as freely as Black Hambro, and requires similar treatment, except that the leaves ought to be moved aside to allow the sun to act upon the fruit, which will greatly enhance the colour. Obtained by crossing Black Morocco and White Sweetwater. Bunches large, compact, and tapering; berries medium, oval; skin pale-yellow, or greenish when not properly finished; flesh tender, melting, juicy, with a rich saccharine flavour.

FRANKENTHAL BLACK HAMBRO (Victoria Hambro, Black Tripoli).—Considered by some to be identical with Black Hambro, but it is quite distinct, having larger round berries and a much more robust habit. Bunch large and heavily shouldered; skin black when well coloured, well bloomed, thicker than Black Hambro, which fact enables the grower to keep this Grape until Christmas if needed; flesh firm, juicy, sugary, and good-flavoured; growth vigorous, and very productive. A noble Grape.

GOLDEN CHAMPION.—A handsome but uncertain Grape. Should be worked on the Black Hambro to impart vigour to its weak constitution, and grown either on the long-rod or long-spur principle to ensure fruitfulness. Bunches large, shouldered; berries very large, oval; skin thin, pale-yellow; flesh firm, juicy, with a Sweetwater flavour. Its proper position is in the list of early varieties. Was raised by the late Mr. W. Thomson at Dalkeith.

GOLDEN QUEEN. — This fine Grape is much esteemed by some cultivators. On some soils it is a great success, but requires Muscat treatment to bring out its best points. Bunches long, tapering, shouldered; berries oblong or oval, an inch or more in length, on rather long stalks;

skin membranous, amber-coloured; flesh firm, juicy, and richly flavoured. Will keep on the canes until the end of the year.

GRIZZLY FRONTIGNAN (Red Frontignan).—In foliage, form of bunch and of berries, this variety

system to secure a sufficiency of bunches, or otherwise grown on the long-rod principle for the same reason. A bunch grown by Mr. Roberts of Charleville Forest, Ireland, weighed 23 lb. 5 oz.

GROS MAROC (Cooper's Late Black) (fig. 30).—

Fig. 28.—Grape—Foster's Seedling

is similar to Black Frontignan, and its rich Muscat flavour is also much the same, the only material difference being the colour. Some consider the Red Frontignan different, but we think the supposed difference arises from the Grizzly becoming, under some circumstances, more red than usual, or from the Black Frontignan colouring only red instead of black, as is sometimes the case with Black Hambro. Introduced by Sir William Temple about 200 years ago. The Black, the White, and the Grizzly Frontignan all require the same treatment.

GROS COLMAN (Gros Colmar). — Bunch of medium length, sometimes long, shoulders broad, the latter often being of nearly the same size as the bunch; a very free setter; berries very large, oval; skin thick, black, well covered with bloom when properly finished; flesh coarse, juicy, sweet when well ripened, otherwise of an indifferent flavour much resembling that of a Mulberry. It is a late Grape, and if worked on Muscat of Alexandria and accorded Muscat treatment the flavour is much improved; requires considerable time to finish. The Vine is a vigorous grower, very fruitful, and is one of the best to grow for market, where appearance is of paramount importance. The thinning of the berries must be done early and with a free hand, to allow of the full development of those retained.

GROS GUILLAUME (Seacliff Black, Barbarossa of some) (fig. 29).—Strong grower, rather shy in bearing. Leaves large and downy. Bunch very large, tapering, and shouldered; berries large, somewhat oval, black, bloom thin; skin tough; flesh tender and juicy, agreeably but not richly flavoured. It is a valuable late Grape, hanging till March, and it is only after hanging thus that it attains its best condition. The Vine, like nearly all other late kinds, delights in Muscat treatment; should be pruned on the long-spur

Bunches large, long, compact, and evenly shouldered; berries very large, roundish-oval; skin thick, black, and covered with dense bluish-grey bloom;

Fig. 29.—Grape—Gros Guillaume (Barbarossa)

flesh tender, sweet; flavour pleasant, but not rich. The Vine is a vigorous grower, but must not be too closely pruned if first-rate bunches are desired. Some growers advise it being grown on the long-rod system to produce the best results. Succeeds and ripens with Black Hambro, and hangs well till the end of the year. Is a mid-season variety of easy cultivation, and may be grown where Gros Colman is not a success.

Fig. 30.—Grape—Gros Maroc

LADY DOWNES (Lady Downes's Seedling) (fig. 31).—A most valuable late-keeping Grape, surpassing all others in this respect, as it will hang without decay, loss of colour, or plumpness till

the fault of scalding badly, to counteract which less moisture should be given, keeping the hot-water pipes warm throughout the night, and leaving the ventilators slightly open during the stoning period. Bunches oblong, with generally an irregular-shaped shoulder, which most growers remove; berries large, roundish-oval; skin thickish, membranous, of a purplish-black, becoming quite black when fully coloured, and covered with a good bloom; flesh firm, richly flavoured, and excellent. The wood and leaves are downy, and the foliage is remarkably handsome in the autumn.

LADY HUTT.—A large, round, white Sweetwater Grape of the highest merit; is a good keeper, and when better known will be largely cultivated for late supply. Foliage and habit of growth similar to Gros Colman; the leaves become pale-yellow in autumn. Bunch medium to large, shouldered, compact; berries large, round; skin thin, greenish-yellow at first, afterwards changing to pale-amber; flesh tender, juicy, breaking, and richly flavoured. Should be grown with Lady Downes, as it requires a long season of growth in which to properly mature its fruit. Will then keep in the Grape-room in fine condition till March. Was raised at Appley Towers, Isle of Wight.

LADY HASTINGS.—A shoot from Muscat Ham'bro. Bunches long, tapering; berries very large, oval; skin black, covered with a dense bloom; flesh crisp, juicy, with a rich Muscat flavour. Is a vigorous grower, sets freely, and is recommended to be grafted on Black Hambro and grown on the extension principle. Ripens in advance of Black Hambro.

MADRESFIELD COURT. — Bunches large, long,

Fig. 31.—Grape—Lady Downes

the end of March, if thoroughly ripened and accorded proper treatment. It is slow to start into growth, and on that account should be started not later than mid-March, in order that its fruits may be mature by the beginning of October. It succeeds best on its own roots, and when given the same treatment as is afforded Muscats. The Vine is vigorous and fruitful, but the berries have

tapering, sometimes widely shouldered, with a short stalk; skin tough but not thick, black, covered with a blue bloom; berries large, oval, or oblong; footstalks short and stout; flesh tender and juicy, rich, with a true Muscat flavour. This is a very excellent early Grape of great merit; will succeed in a cool vinery. Should be grown with the early or mid-season varieties, it being a failure in the late vinery. In some places the berries crack during the ripening process, to obviate which a current of warm dry air should be kept constantly circulating through the house. Air should therefore be admitted by both the top and front ventilators day and night, and the hot-water pipes always kept warmed. Also cover down inside borders to prevent damp rising, and place shutters or something similar to shed rain off outer borders.

MELTON CONSTABLE. — A fine valuable late-keeping Grape; one of the best for market. Bunches medium-sized, much like Gros Colmar; berries very large, round, black, densely bloomed; skin thin; flesh crisp, flavour sweet and pleasant. Should be grown with the latest varieties and given Muscat treatment. Is vigorous and fruitful.

late vinery. Bunches medium to large, broad-shouldered, tapering; berries roundish-oval; skin thick, amber-coloured when fully ripe; pulp firm, juicy, sugary, with a Muscat flavour. Raised by Mr. Pearson of Chilwell from Black Alicante, crossed with Ferdinand de Lesseps.

MRS. PINCE'S BLACK MUSCAT. — Bunches large, very long and tapering, shouldered, with a short stalk; berries oval, medium sized, with short, stout stalks; skin tough, thick, blackish purple, seldom well-coloured; bloom moderate in density; flesh firm, with a decided Muscat flavour. A useful late-keeping Grape, requiring time and a high temperature to finish it to perfection. It is best grown on its own roots, and should be fertilized by hand when in flower, when it sets abundantly.

Fig. 32.—Muscat of Alexandria

MILLER'S BURGUNDY. — Leaves downy, nearly white, in allusion to which appearance it has the name of Miller Grape, or one with that signification, in various languages. Bunches short, ovate, compact; berries small, round or inclining to roundish-oval; skin thin, black; flesh tender, with an abundance of juice, which is rather sharp after the fruit is coloured, and when fully ripe is not so sweet as the Black Cluster. It is hardy, and therefore suited for cultivation against a wall in the open air.

MILL HILL HAMBRO. — Leaves large, pale yellowish-green, flaccid. Bunches large, long, and well shouldered; berries large, round, inclining to oblate, dented as if hammered; skin black, covered with blue bloom, thin and tender; flesh melting and tender, juicy, sweet, and richly flavoured. A noble-looking Grape of excellent quality, but does not keep long after it is ripe.

MRS. PEARSON.—Although not generally cultivated, this Grape finds favour with some by whom it is well grown. It is a round white Grape possessing a Muscat flavour; a good setter and keeper, and should be accorded a warm position in the

MUSCAT CHAMPION.—Leaves and general habit of growth much resembling Mill Hill Hambro, which was one of its parents. Bunches large and well-shouldered; berries large, round; skin red or grizzly; flesh tender, rich, with the distinct flavour peculiar to the Frontignans. A mid-season Grape, succeeding in a greenhouse vinery, but is not often cultivated.

MUSCAT OF ALEXANDRIA (Charlesworth Tokay) (fig. 32). — Vine vigorous, of robust growth. Leaves large, deeply lobed, sharply serrated, smooth above, slightly pubescent beneath; petioles long, smooth, stained with red, as are also the ribs some distance from them. Bunches large, tapering, strongly shouldered; berries large, oval, hanging loosely; skin rather thick, of a pale-amber colour, with a rather thin bloom; flesh firm and breaking, exceedingly rich, with a very pronounced and delicious musk-like flavour. Succeeds best when grown in a house by itself. If it has to be accommodated in a mixed house, it should be with such varieties as require strong heat, or what is termed Muscat treatment. Requires particular care in the setting, this having to be done with the pollen of the Hambro or a similar free-setting kind in many places, to ensure good and shapely examples. A higher degree of temperature is requisite to thoroughly ripen the fruit and ensure that rich amber tint so much admired in well-finished samples of this Grape. Exposing the berries to direct sunlight is also a great aid in securing depth of colour.

PRINCE OF WALES.—A first-rate late-keeping Grape. Vine vigorous and fruitful. Leaves large, and unless lightly shaded are apt to "scald". Bunches large, tapering, with stout stalk; berries oval, very large, purple-black, coated with grey bloom; skin thin; flesh tender, has a rich Muscat flavour. As it takes a long time to colour, it should be given Muscat treatment and grown with Lady Downes and other heat-loving varieties. Being a shy setter, it is necessary to resort to artificial fertilization.

REINE OLGA.—One of the best varieties to grow in the open air. Bunches large, tapering; berries medium-sized, round; skin thin, red, thinly bloomed; flesh melting, with a Sweetwater flavour. Best grown on the extension system.

ROYAL MUSCADINE (Chasselas).—Leaves with moderately deep lobes, smooth above and almost so beneath; the under side thickly reticulated. Bunches medium, tapering, occasionally shouldered; berries medium, round; skin thin, white-amber; flesh tender, rich, and sugary. A good bearer and sets well. One of the best white Grapes for the open wall, greenhouse, and for early forcing in pots.

SYRIAN.—Bunch very large with broad shoulders; berries large, oval; skin thick, white; flesh firm, of tolerable flavour when well ripened in strong heat to a fine amber colour. Not recommended for a limited collection, one Vine sufficing for a large establishment. Grown by Mr. Speechly, at Welbeck, in 1781, to a weight of 19½ lb.

TREBBIANO.—Bunch very large, long, broad-shouldered and well set; berries roundish-oval, medium, on short stalks; skin thick, greenish-yellow, becoming amber-coloured when properly finished; flesh firm, juicy, sweet, but not rich. Requires a long season of growth and Muscat treatment to bring out its best qualities. A handsome Grape, valuable on account of its long-keeping properties. Some remarkably fine bunches have been produced at different times by noted growers, Mr. Curror, of Eskbank, having grown it to a weight of 26¼ lb.

TRENTHAM BLACK.—Leaves bluntly lobed, dark-green, and of thick texture. Bunches tapering, shouldered; berries medium, roundish-oval; skin thin but tough, separating freely from the pulp, black, with a copious bloom; flesh juicy, rich, and vinous. Bears forcing well, ripening as early as Black Hambro. A very capricious Grape, but of excellent flavour.

WEST'S ST. PETERS.—Leaves acutely serrated, cordate at the base, glabrous, with the exception of a slight pubescence on the ribs; when fading, the leaves assume a purplish-crimson hue. Bunch medium, sometimes large and broad-shouldered; berries round, inclining to oval; skin rather thin, black, with a fine bloom; flesh purplish, sugary, and rich. An excellent Grape for invalids. The variety is a good bearer, and valuable on account of its late-keeping properties. Should be grown with Lady Downes and other varieties which require a high temperature, and be started not later than the middle of March, so that the fruit may become ripe before the leaves begin to fade. It will then keep well into the next year.

WHITE FRONTIGNAN.—Growth free. Leaves roundish, open at the base, not deeply (sometimes scarcely) lobed, but having deep serratures; mid-rib not bristly. Bunches long, conical; berries middle-sized, round; skin white; flesh somewhat thinner than that of Royal Muscadine, and possessing a rich delicious Muscat flavour. In the South of England it will in some seasons ripen tolerably well on an outer wall. It can be grown to perfection in a vinery with Black Hambro, and is worthy of cultivation on account of its rich flavour.

WHITE NICE.—A very old, second-rate Grape, seldom cultivated at the present day. Its proper place is in the latest vinery, as the fruit requires a considerable length of time in which to finish properly. Leaves very downy beneath. Bunch very large and loose; berries medium, somewhat oval; skin rather thin, greenish-white, pale-amber when ripe; pulp tolerably soft and juicy, but not rich. Mr. Dickson, of Arkleton, excelled in growing large bunches of this variety, the heaviest weighing 25 lb. 15 oz.

WHITE TOKAY.—An excellent late white Grape of far better quality than either Trebbiano or Calabrian Raisin. Should be grown in the coolest end of the vinery; and the fruit is best cut and transferred to the Grape-room as soon as the Vine has shed its leaves. Bunch medium to large, broad-shouldered; skin thick, rich-amber colour when highly finished; flesh firm and agreeably flavoured. Will keep a long time in excellent condition if well ripened before being cut.

SELECTION OF SORTS

For Walls in the Open Air.

Black Hambro.	Miller's Burgundy.
Chasselas Vibert.	Reine Olga.
Gamay Noir.	Royal Muscadine.

For Cool Vinery

Black Hambro.	Madresfield Court.
Foster's Seedling.	Royal Muscadine.

For Early Forcing

Black Hambro.	Lady Hastings.
Buckland Sweetwater.	Madresfield Court.
Duke of Buccleuch.	Royal Muscadine.
Foster's Seedling.	

For a Mid-season Vinery

Alicante.	Foster's Seedling.
Black Hambro.	Gros Maroc.
Buckland Sweetwater.	Madresfield Court.
Diamond Jubilee.	

SELECTION OF SORTS

For a Muscat Vinery

Bowood Muscat.
Mrs. Pearson.
Mrs. Pince's Black Muscat.

Muscat Champion.
Muscat of Alexandria.
Prince of Wales.

For Forcing in Pots

Alicante.
Black Hambro.
Foster's Seedling.

Madresfield Court.
Royal Muscadine.

For a Late Vinery

Alicante.
Alnwick Seedling.
Appley Towers.
Chasselas Napoleon.
Diamond Jubilee.
Gros Colman.
Gros Guillaume.
Lady Downes.

Lady Hutt.
Mrs. Pince's Black Muscat.
Melton Constable.
Muscat of Alexandria.
Prince of Wales.
White Tokay.

For Exhibition

Alicante.
Alnwick Seedling.
Appley Towers.
Black Hambro.
Bowood Muscat.
Chasselas Napoleon.
Directeur Tisserand.
Foster's Seedling.
Golden Queen.

Gros Colman.
Gros Guillaume.
Gros Maroc.
Lady Downes.
Madresfield Court.
Melton Constable.
Muscat of Alexandria.
Prince of Wales.
Trebbiano.

Printed in Great Britain
by Amazon